A Healthy Body

By Julie Haydon

T0362643

Contents

Be Healthy

Everyone wants to be healthy.
People who are healthy feel good and look good.

Food

Healthy people eat good food every day and rarely eat junk food.

Water

Healthy people drink lots of water every day. They do not drink soft drinks very often.

Exercise

Healthy people do lots of exercise every week. They do not watch television for hours every day.

Sleep

Healthy people get lots of sleep and do not stay up late very often.

Keep Clean

Healthy people keep their bodies clean.
They clean their skin, their hair and their teeth.
Healthy people do not go to bed
without brushing their teeth.

Protect the Body

Healthy people take care of their bodies.

Healthy people protect their bodies from the weather, from accidents, and from danger.

Your Brain and Heart

Your brain and your heart
are important parts of your body.

Your brain and heart are inside your body.

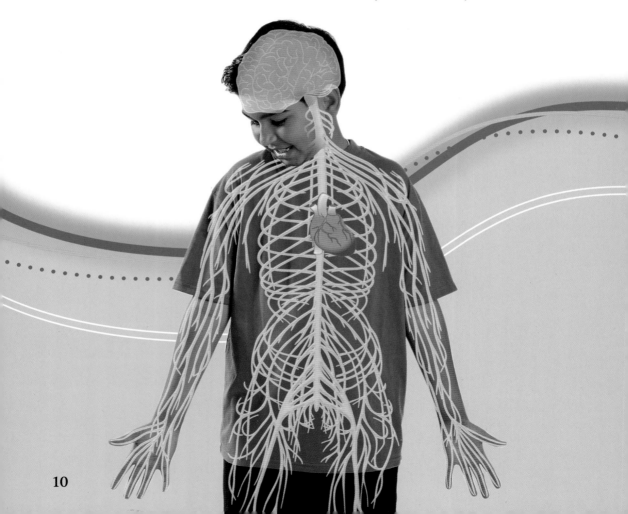

10

Your Brain

Your brain is inside your head.
It is protected by your skull.

Your brain looks like a huge, fleshy walnut.

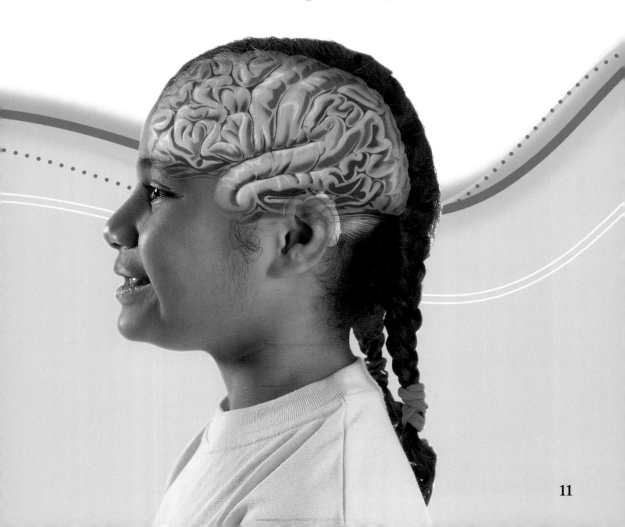

Your brain does many things.
It learns new information and skills,
and can remember many things.

Your brain also gets messages from your senses
and works out what the messages mean.

sight

touch

hearing

taste

smell

Your brain helps you move
and keep your balance.

Your brain keeps your heart beating
at the right speed
even when you are sleeping.

Your Heart

Your heart is a strong muscle in your chest.
It is protected by your ribs.

Your heart is a little bit bigger than your fist.

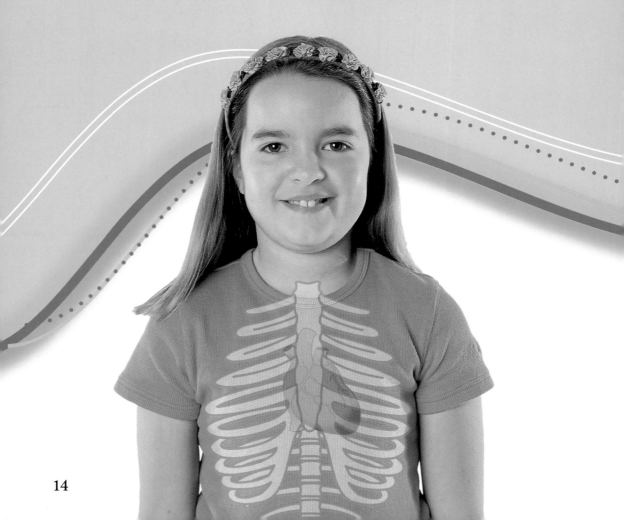

Your heart pumps blood around your body.
Your heart beats all through your life.

It beats quickly when you are exercising.
It beats more slowly when you are resting.

Even though you cannot see your brain and heart,
they are always working.

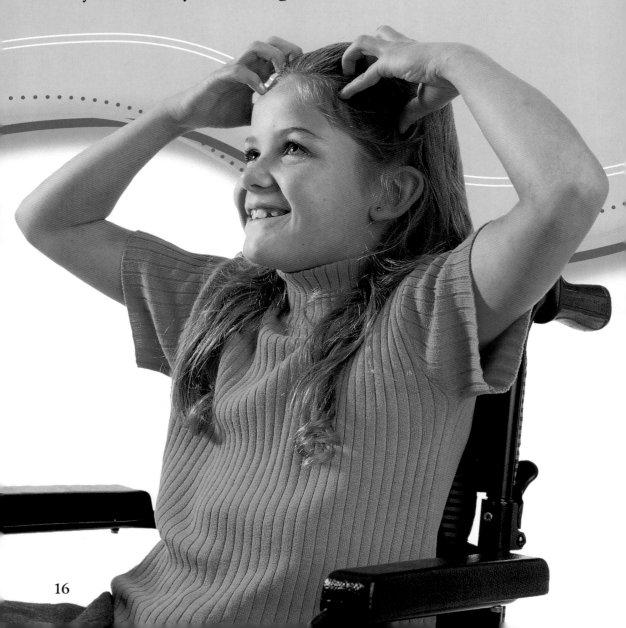